The Mantle of Ministry

The Mantle of Ministry

OF

Embracing the Call

Joyce Myrick Wooden

XULON PRESS

Xulon Press
2301 Lucien Way #415
Maitland, FL 32751
407.339.4217

www.xulonpress.com

© 2020 by Joyce Myrick Wooden

All rights reserved solely by the author. The author guarantees all contents are original and do not infringe upon the legal rights of any other person or work. No part of this book may be reproduced in any form without the permission of the author. The views expressed in this book are not necessarily those of the publisher.

Words of inspiration included from poster "*If Asked the Question, Who Are We Tell Them We Are From A-Z*" copy written in 1983.

Unless otherwise indicated, Scripture quotations taken from the King James Version (KJV) – *public domain.*

Scripture quotations taken from the New King James Version (NKJV). Copyright © 1982 by Thomas Nelson, Inc. Used by permission. All rights reserved.

Printed in the United States of America

Paperback ISBN-13: 978-1-6322-1353-2
Ebook ISBN-13: 978-1-6322-1354-9

Content

SECTION 1: AN ESSENCE OF WHO WE ARE! 1
    Introduction 3
    The Mantle of Ministry.................................. 5
    The Mantle Is the Bestowing of Ministry Gifts 7
    Bridging the Old and the New 9
    Designed with You in Mind 11
    Accepting Our Undistorted Identity, Affirmation, and
        Reinstatement 15
    Affirmation of Confirmation on Our Identity in Christ 16
    In Occurrence with Divine Order 18
    The Great Call, the Equipping and Sending 20

**SECTION 2: WE ARE COMMITTED TO THE CAUSE AND THE
    CALL OUR ANSWER TO GOD IS YES!** 25
    Gifts to the Body The Ascension Gifts Given by Christ 27
    The Mantle of Apostle.................................. 30
    The Mantle of Prophet 34
    The Mantle of Evangelist 38
    The Mantle of Pastor—Teacher........................... 39

**SECTION 3: WE ARE EXAMPLES OF GOD'S GRACE
    AND MERCY!**.. 43
    The Overseer and Bishop 45

**SECTION 4: WE ARE THE LIGHTS BY WHICH OTHER
    FIND GOD!** 51
    The Elders... 53
    The Charge to the Elder 56
    Within the Local Assembly, the Role of the Missionary 58

Section 5: We Are Committed and Rewarded For Our Faithfulness to God! 63
  Recognizing the Call..65

Section 6: We Walk By Faith We Serve by God's Grace..71
  God Is a God of Order and Governing Power 73

Section 7: We Are Motivated to Follow Through in God's Work and Deeds! 75
  More than Apparel Appeal 77
  Workers Together with Him Minters and Conduits of Grace..79
  The Qualifications of the Called............................81
  An Effective Leader 83
  The Necessity of Preparation...............................87
  Entry and Recommended Course Requirements 89

Section 1

An Essence of Who We Are!

We are all special
We are all similar,
Yet exceptionally different in our way!
We were born for a purpose,
Sent here to fulfill God's plan
To bring salvation and redemption
Also, to restore fallen man!

Yes, we are all special
We are all similar,
We are inadvertently (purposefully) unique
Sent here to make a change for God
In our own inimitable, and individual, yet individually distinct way!

Joyce Myrick Wooden, 2011

INTRODUCTION

And I sought for a man among them, that should make up the hedge, and stand in the gap before me for the land, that I should not destroy it: but I found none. Ezekiel 22:30 (KJV)

God is still looking for the one who will make up the hedge of protection and the one who will stand in the gap. He is still looking and calling for the one who will become the bridge for others to cross from darkness to light. The call is great, but who will answer?

This book offers guidance and information to the many men and women engaged in the work of ministry. In over thirty years of ministry and working in one capacity and then another, I have met many interesting people who make up the family of God, each equipped with unique gifts, skills, and abilities. With this, I have heard and seen many points of view or opinions, and as a result, many things transpired.

As I listened to others, I have had the opportunity of hearing numerous ideas concerning women who feel duty-bound to answer the call to ministry. It is sad to say that there has been so much (in many instances, underserved, as well as perhaps unintentional) abuse in this area by words spoken or actions performed. It is, therefore, with sincere prayer and heartfelt desire that this instrument of Nuggets' *The Mantel of Ministry Embracing the Call*, is presented. These are to guide toward a more comprehensive understanding of what it is to be called and chosen by God for the unique and extraordinary work of the ministry, and all that it entails regardless of gender, or moral status or background.

In saying this, it is vital that you the reader will view *The Mantle of Ministry* as a process of preparation for present and succeeding generations through the impartation and unction of the Holy Spirit, by equipping, teaching, empowering, commissioning, authorizing, and covering for active ministry. Also, the information herein is to motivate and enhance the anointed competent minister to be all God has called you to be in Him and the work of His ministry.

The effort herein is to offer guidance and information that will enhance and motivate both genders on each side of the continuum. As both male and female, created in His image, we hold the precise purpose of giving God complete preeminence and glory from, for, and within the lives He has entrusted to us. I humbly encourage all to open their minds to glean a higher, more in-depth understanding. With that, I encourage you to aim to reach high and to go far beyond what these pages offer and that you become most effective in all you endeavor to do for the upbuilding of God's kingdom work in the earth and for His Glory!

The Mantle Of Ministry

Many may be asking what the mantel is—more specifically, what is the mantle of ministry? The word *mantle*, which appears in the Hebrew and Aramaic language in which the Old Testament is composed, is described as a garment of glory, a goodly robe, a cloak, or coat. Thus, the mantle was a wrap, a piece of fabric with a distinct design. Throughout ancient history, a variety of people from varying positions wore it. In many situations, it represented the anointed investment of the office of the prophet. Also, the wearing of the mantle as a garment extends from at least the time of the Exodus by both male and female prophets and prophetess of that day.

In the Book of 2 Kings, the prophet Elijah introduces us to the transferring of the mantle to Elisha. The transference of the mantle, initiated by Almighty God, signified the actual act of the passing of prophetic responsibility and His accompanying power and of bestowing of the gift from one to another. As seen with Elijah and Elisha, exceptional skill and anointing were transferred from one individual to the next through the garment referred to as the mantle. We have come to know that this power and anointing does not reside in a piece of fabric but rather in the spirit of individuals chosen by God whom He desires to bestow such gifts, abilities, and anointing upon those called to ministry.

The Mantle Is The Bestowing Of Ministry Gifts

Christ in equipping the church for edification, Himself bestowed the Mantle of Ministry in five distinct areas—apostle, prophet, evangelist, pastor, and teacher—upon the believer through the ascension gifts Paul identifies in Ephesians 4:8 and 13:

> Wherefore He saith, When He ascended on high, He led captivity captive, and gave gifts unto men," Till we all come in the unity of the faith, and the knowledge of the Son of God, unto a perfect man, unto the measure of the stature of the fullness of Christ.

The Mantle of Ministry in these last days of the church age is broad and therefore encases the fivefold ministry in its entirety, with the focus of edifying and building up the body of Christ until we the believers in Christ come to our full statue and maturity in Him. The Mantle of Ministry is, therefore, our investment or the investiture worn by those called to ministry with specific gifting, talents, and attributes, which are for the utilization for ministry purpose as we accomplish our assignment in the earth as mandated by God from the beginning (Gen. 1: 26–28 and Eph. 4:11–13).

This Mantle of Ministry, therefore, comes without any restrictions of gender. Whether we are male or female, Greek (Gentile) or Jew, we are one and are designed with and for a specific purpose. We are the instruments, endowed with special anointing, appointed to works, and assigned to the body of Christ for the saving and perseverance of humankind.

Bridging The Old To The New

Joel prophesied,

> Moreover, it shall come to pass afterward, that I will pour out my spirit upon all flesh; and your sons and your daughters shall prophesy, your old men shall dream dreams, your young men shall see visions: And also upon the servants and upon the handmaids in those days will I pour out my spirit. (Joel 2:28–29 KJV)

The Book of Acts refers to the prophecy given by the prophet Joel, in which the Holy Spirit on the day of Pentecost fulfilled the promise made. Acts 2:14–18 thus states,

> However, this is that which was spoken by the prophet Joel; And it shall come to pass in the last days, saith God, I will pour out of my Spirit upon all flesh: and your sons and your daughters shall prophesy. Your young men shall see visions, and your old men shall dream dreams: Moreover, on my servants and my handmaidens, I will pour out in those days of my Spirit; and they shall prophesy. (Acts 2:14–18 KJV)

Designed With You In Mind

Engaging in Ministry

Know Your Self-worth

Knowing your purpose is vital to understand who you are, your self-worth, and your assignment in life. My prayer is that if nothing else, by the end of this book, you will know fully that you were born for a purpose and as a part of a plan by God's design. You were born for this. The "this" could be a preacher, a teacher, a judge, a firefighter, or a concert pianist. However, it is your destiny to do what He has called you out of the darkness and into His marvelous light to do. You are unique and chosen. The things that have happened to this point in your life all happened to you for the preparation of the work He has called you to do. God has your destination in His plans, and He will direct your course in life if you will only allow Him.

You Are Not an Afterthought in the Mind of God

You are His, chosen for such a purpose and such a time as this. As stated by Peter, "But ye are a chosen generation, a royal priesthood, a holy nation, a peculiar people; that ye should shew forth the praises of him who hath called you out of darkness into his marvelous light" (1 Pet. 2:9 KJV). You are a byproduct designed especially by his hands, to give Him adoration and glory. You must know that before your conception, and before you developed in your mother's womb, God saw you. Then, as a little child, while you were yet running around, perhaps barefoot and playing in the yard with other children, through the crowd, God saw you. You are not an afterthought in the mind of God.

You see, it didn't just happen when you acknowledged the Lord and got saved, but it was purposed for you from the beginning of time, before you were born, that you would be His, that you had a unique work to do just for Him. As stated in the Gospel of John, "Ye have not chosen me, but I have chosen you, and ordained you, that ye should go and bring forth fruit, and that your fruit should remain" (John 15:16).

Most assuredly, you were born for this. From the foundation, through generations, God saw you. All of this is your purpose for being here, that you would be His, that you had work to do just for Him. You are here for this purpose. The word of the Lord, as stated in Jeremiah 1:4–10,

> Then the word of the Lord came unto me, saying, Before I formed thee in the belly, I knew thee, and before thou camest forth out of the womb I sanctified thee, and I ordained thee a prophet unto the nations. Then said I, Ah, Lord GOD! Behold, I cannot speak for I am a child. But the Lord said unto me, Say not, I am a child: for thou shalt go to all that I shall send thee, and whatsoever I command thee thou shalt speak. Be not afraid of their faces: for I am with thee to deliver thee, saith the Lord. Then the Lord put forth his hand and touched my mouth. And the Lord said unto me, Behold, I have put my words in thy mouth. See, I have this day set thee over the nations and over the kingdoms, to root out, and to pull down, and to destroy, and to throw down, to build, and to plant.

No Abusiveness Concerning You

God does not intend, nor will He allow, the exploitation of your gifts, skills, and abilities. Your purpose is not merely to build other men's visions but to bring Him glory. Not everyone's intentions are honest and truthful toward ministry work. There are those who are all about the money and will exploit innocent good, hard-working, good-intentioned Christians to reach their desired goals. Paul warns us to be aware of counterfeits who proclaim to be ministers of the Lord. You are not a prostitute to be pimped by men or women under misguided leadership. God will not permit your exploitation by others, and He never uses but utilizes your gifts and abilities to His glory and rewards you faithfully.

The Trails of Preparation and Perfection

Yes, many of you may have gone through unbearable obstacles in life. I understand that even in the church, well-meaning, good-hearted people have suffered unthinkable abuses, have been misunderstood, and, in a sense, have felt trampled on. There are things that many of you have gone through that you probably would never wish on your worst enemy. There are things that many have thought they would never have to endure in life. For those of you who have suffered in various areas that you probably do not even feel free to talk about, there is still hope and purpose for you.

Although you may at times feel hopeless and in despair, God says, give Him a chance to help you come through and overcome your traumatic endeavors: "I will rectify the wrongs in your life. I will cause the sun (My Son) to shine upon you and make your life worth living and successful." If your experience will allow, God will turn your bad into good and your hurt and pain into triumph and will use it toward your preparation for this work.

Know this as truth: God has a purpose for you. However, more importantly, you need Him! Yes, trials and tribulations can be hard. The things that have happened in your life up to this point all happened for a good reason. You were designed by His hands for His purpose and chosen for such use and such a time as this (1 Pet. 2:9). He did not bring you to this point to leave you, and what you have gone through is not in vain.

GOD VALUES YOU

It is with high regard that God has chosen to give you as a gift for His glory for ministry work. God never uses or misuses that which is His. He loves, appreciates, and esteems you to the highest, so do not take His goodness and blessedness for granted. To God be the glory forever. Hallelujah!

Accepting Our Undistorted Identity, Affirmation, And Reinstatment

Yes, it is true, humankind failed in the garden, and women played a pivotal role in the fall, but God has not eternally and ultimately stripped her for this act, nor has God eternally stripped man. Instead, He implemented an antidote for their situation to reinstate them to their position to fulfill His plan and purpose in and through them.

To adequately fulfill this purpose, we must first be affirmed (both male and female), and that affirmation comes through the word of God, which is through the sacrificial Lamb, Jesus Christ, and His atoning death on the cross and resurrection from the dead for our sins. For the scripture says, "That if thou shalt confess with thy mouth the Lord Jesus, and shalt believe in thine heart that God hath raised him from the dead, thou shalt be saved" (Rom. 10:9, KJV).

Our reinstatement with God through Christ brings us back into right standing and in the proper position. God made both the male and female in His image for the purpose of cohabitation, to jointly share in dominion over all things in the earth and to reproduce its kind. The role of a woman, in terms of a more adequately defining the word *help-meet,* is to share complementary to a man in all things of God. When we fail to look at the role, position, and place of the two from this perspective, we come away with a distorted view.

Affirmation Of Confirmation On Our Identity In Christ

Daily we are to remind ourselves that we are:

Accepted by Christ and adopted into the royal family of God, we have been granted the ability to do all things. By abiding in Christ and His words abiding in us, we have access to God. Through the suffering of afflictions, we can learn the abundance of God's mercy, and by acknowledging His ways, which are so different from ours, we find His grace. Having no ambition to see ourselves great, Jesus gave us the authority of edification and made us ambassadors for Christ.

Why? Because we have been:

Bought with the price that Jesus paid while we were yet in our sins, we were made whole. After hearing believing and receiving the wonderful words of God, we repented. We received forgiveness of our sins and our iniquities were blotted out. We were then baptized according to our faith through the water baptism and received the seal of our new birth through the baptism of the Holy Ghost.

Further, our calling and affirmation come from God alone, for we are:

Called of God, we now press toward the prize of the higher calling of God in Christ Jesus. We have confidence in God that we will make it through. We are comforted with this throughout. God cares for us. By having our hearts cleansed and our minds made up, we can do all things through Christ who strengthens us, for we have been made more than conquerors through His love (Wooden, 1983).

In Occurrence With Divine Order

There is something else of relevance that we must be mindful of concerning women engaging in ministry. We would be amiss not to admit that because of the fall, many things are out of order. Although our identity is established and affirmed as daughters in an equal relationship with our male counterparts and that we are not afterthoughts in the mind of God as some would have us to believe, there is still a divine order of things.

Proper Respect to the Headship in the Home

There is a fact that not every woman has a husband. As a result, there are cases wherein women are heads of families because of absentee fathers in many of our homes. However, in lines of proper positioning where there is a husband and wife, family, Christian wives, and children should give appropriate respect to the headship in the household.

Women In Leadership Position: Home, Work, And Church

Besides, there are occasions where women are in leadership in their jobs or in their careers, which includes the church. These women can operate in these capacities as adequately as any man does because God made and equipped them to do so. A great biblical example of this is Deborah, found in Judges, the fourth chapter. Also, on many occasions, where Priscilla's and Aquila's names appear in the Bible, Pricilla's name is usually mentioned first, which was due to the pivotal role of leadership. She, along with her husband, was very instrumental in working with the apostle Paul and the establishing of the first-century church.

There are many other women in leadership, such as Esther, Miriam, and the prophetess and judge Deborah, just to name a few.

THE GREAT CALL, THE EQUIPPING AND SENDING

Scripture clearly states that before ascending to heaven, Jesus placed things in order by calling forth those in whom He would invest Himself in to establish His work on earth. These individuals would become what we have come to know as His original apostles. Their purpose would be to go forth to preach, to heal the sick, and to cast out devils/unclean spirits.

In Mark 3:13–15 we see Jesus as he goes up into a mountain. Once there, he calls the twelve who have engaged in ministry for the last three-and a-half years. He ordains and empowers each of them, sending them into the world to preach the gospel, to heal those that are sick, and to free (liberate) those tormented and bound by devils and all unclean spirits. Among these twelve disciples in alphabetical order were:

Andrew

Andrew was the brother of Simon Peter and one of the apostles of Jesus. Andrew was born in Bethsaida of Galilee and of course, by profession, was originally a fisherman. Andrew played a pivotal role in leading many to Christ, but unlike his brother Simon Peter and others, little is mentioned of him after the formation of the early church.

Bartholomew/Nathanael

Bartholomew was an Israelite, whose name is also believed to have been Nathanael. He was also one of the twelve original apostles of Jesus. Bartholomew is mentioned in the Synoptic Gospels along with Philip. However, he is not mentioned by the name Nathanael. Bartholomew/Nathanael was present at the appearing of Jesus, at the Sea of Tiberias as seen in John 21:2, and he was a witness of our Lord Jesus's ascension in Acts chapter one.

James, the Elder

The Elder or the Greater was also one of the original twelve apostles of Jesus. He was the son of Zebedee and Salome and was born in Bethsaida. Salome, James's mother, was a sister of Mary, the mother of Jesus, making them first cousins. He was one of the inner circle members of Jesus.

James, the Lesser or Younger

James the Younger or Lesser, and in some places called the Minor, is one of the twelve original apostles. He was chosen by Jesus and is not the son of Zebedee. However, he is the brother of Mathew, the apostle of Jesus.

John

There is much to be learned about the apostle John. He was the son of Zebedee and Salome, brother of James the Elder and first cousin of Jesus our Lord. He was one of the members of the inner circle with Jesus and was seated with Him at the Last Supper. He was at the crucifixion with Mary, the mother of Jesus, his aunt, and given charge of her care. He is the author of the Gospel of John; the first, second, and third epistles; and the book of Revelation. He is the longest living of the original apostles and endured many horrific things during his life for the name's sake of Christ. He addressed the body of Christ as "dearly beloved" and reminds us that "love is of God and everyone that loveth is born of God, for God is love, so beloved let us love one another." (1 John 4:7–9, KJV)

Judas

Judas's name Iscariot is most likely associated with the region or town he came from, Queriot or Kerioth. He became one of the twelve apostles and carried the money purse. He became notoriously known as the betrayer after selling Christ out to the Sanhedrin for thirty pieces of silver, which at that time amounted to approximately six hundred dollars.

Jud /Thaddeus

Jude, also known as Thaddeus, was one of the original twelve disciples of Jesus. In some places he is named the son of or brother of James; whichever makes for a good study. He was born in Galilee, an Israelite.

Matthew/Levi

Matthew, who was also named Levi, was Jewish and born in Galilee. He worked for the Roman government and was gainfully employed prior to prior to becoming a follower of Christ as a tax collector and was not very well liked by his community. Matthew went on to follow Christ, forsaking much to do so, and became one of the original twelve apostles. Matthew wrote the Gospel of Matthew, giving the real-life account of the life of Christ.

Peter or Simon Peter

Peter, also named Simon, was referred to as Simon bar Jonah, or Cephas, the rock. He is the son of Zebedee and the brother of Andrew. Zebedee and his sons, which included Peter, were fishermen prior to him becoming one of the original twelve apostles. Peter's call to apostleship was pertinent in the formation of the early church. He wore the mantle of apostle well, and there is so much to be learned or studied about this individual. He was present at the mountain of transfiguration, he denied knowing Jesus before His crucifixion, but he was the spokesman on the day of Pentecost and was very prevalent throughout the first fifteen chapters of the Book of Acts. He is the author of two epistles that instruct the church of the day.

Philip

Phillip was born in Bethsaida and is mentioned in the gospels as one of the twelve apostles of Jesus. He is also connected with Andrew and Peter, and they probably knew each other prior to becoming followers of Christ. John's Gospel gives attention to Phillip on various occasions. John mentions him as being the one who asked Jesus how they would feed the multitude of five thousand. Phillip the apostle seen in the gospels is not the same Phillip mentioned in the Book of Acts, the evangelist.

Simon, the Zealot

Simon the Zealot was born in Cana. He was one of the original twelve apostles of Jesus. Not very much is mentioned of him, but he is distinguished from Simon Peter the "Rock." However, he does make for an interesting study.

Thomas

Thomas, also called Didymus, was a twin. He was most famously known as "doubting Thomas. He was a Galilean by birth. Thomas had a distinct personality. He was inquisitive, while on the other hand, doubtful. He was also described as faithful and courageous after being empowered by the Holy Ghost. Thomas is believed to have travelled to India, where he is revered for the extraordinary work he accomplished there before being martyred.

As stated before, some of the original twelve apostles faded into the backgrounds of early church history, and not much is heard about them after the initial recordings in the gospels, such as (Andrew, Bartholomew/Nathanael, Matthew/Levi, or Simon the Zealot, and Thomas).

However, many went on to become well known throughout the early Christian community, such as John, Jude/Thaddeus, Peter or Simon Peter, and Philip. There were two James's, James the Elder and James the Lesser or Younger. One of them became significantly known, but we are not clear about the other. Then there was Judas, the one who betrayed Jesus. His guilt for betraying Jesus was so great that he ended his own life. We learn in the Book of Acts that first, there was a casting of lots for Judas's replacement, which was Matthias. However, the Apostle Paul by the will of God, became the actual replacement for Judas, and nothing is heard of Matthias again.

Section 2

WE ARE COMMITTED TO THE CAUSE AND THE CALL OUR ANSWER TO GOD IS YES!

Words that describe our zeal, devotion, motivation and striving: *Determined* is the word to describe our devotion. Our heart's desire is to diligently seek the Lord. We are dedicated to the true teachings of the doctrine of God, and in it we find the strength needed to overcome sin and death.

Elected of God and edified through His knowledge describes how we are educated daily in His ways. We earnestly seek to do His will, and we put forth every effort possible to get it done. We ever thank God for each other—our sisters and brothers. We always show forth this never-dying love for one another by exhorting each other through the unction and inspiration of the Holy Ghost (Wooden, 1983).

These Are Needed in Our Spiritual Walk!

Commitment:	1 Peter 1:23; 2 Timothy 6:20 and 2 Timothy 2:2
Courage:	Joshua 1:9; 2 Chronicles 15:8 and Ezra 10:4
Faithfulness:	1 John 1:9; 1 Corinthians 10:13, and 1 Thessalonians 5:24
Godliness:	1 Timothy 4:8, 2 Timothy 3:5–7, and 2 Peter 1:3–9
Honesty:	Philippians 4:8,9; Acts 6:3; Hebrews 13:18
Humility:	1 Peter 5:5; 2 Timothy 2:25, and Titus 2:7
Integrity:	Job 2:3; Psalm 41:12, and Titus 2:7
Loyalty:	1 Kings 8:61; 2 Kings 20:3, and Matthew 6:24
Readiness:	Acts 17:11; 1 Timothy 4:13, and 2 Corinthians 8:11
Trustworthiness:	Luke 19:12–26; Psalm 3:5, 6 and Nahum 1:7
Truthfulness:	Proverbs 14:2–5 and Proverbs 12;19–22
Willingness:	Acts 8:26–40, and Isaiah 1:18, 19

Gifts To The Body
The Ascension Gifts Given By Christ

Ephesians 4:11–16 (KJV)

... And he gave some, apostles; and some, prophets; and some, evangelists; and some, pastors and teachers; For the perfecting of the saints, for the work of the ministry, for the edifying of the body of Christ: Till we all come in the unity of the faith, and the knowledge of the Son of God, unto a perfect man, unto the measure of the stature of the fullness of Christ: That we henceforth be no more children, tossed to and fro, and carried about with every wind of doctrine, by the sleight of men, and cunning craftiness, whereby they lie in wait to deceive; But speaking the truth in love, may grow up into him in all things, which is the head, even Christ: From whom the whole body fitly joined together and compacted by that which every joint supplieth, according to the effectual working in the measure of every part, maketh increase of the body unto the edifying of itself in love.

God gave these people to the church as gifts. These people, like gifts, are for those only who declare the gospel and teach the truth. We refer to these as the Mantle of Ministry to the Church, which includes:

Apostles, Prophets, Evangelists, Pastors, and Teachers

Besides these, which will be explained in more detail later, are the bishops, overseers, elders' ministers, and missionaries.

All of these are the ministerial leadership of the local, national, and worldwide church.

In this, God has given every provision needed for every individual that makes up His body, the church. Through these selected individuals, He gives us instruction through His Word and His abiding presence through His Holy Spirit, as well as the love for one another. He gives us faith for victory in our lives, spiritually, physically, mentally, socially, and materially.

He has given these individuals, as we call ministers, as His agents, ambassadors, and assistants. He has given them the authority to preach, exhort, and rebuke, as stated in 2 Timothy 4:1–2. This authority also includes the ministry to teach, admonish, counsel, correct, and encourage.

He gave these individuals, as stated in Ephesians, the fourth chapter "for the perfecting of the saints" (Eph. 4:11–17). From this view, which is an accurate one, a Christian must have these individuals at work in their life for perfection. Let us look at the ministry of Apostle Paul, Barnabas, and others:

Galatians 1:1 (KJV):

> "Paul, an apostle, (not of men, neither by man, but by Jesus Christ, and God the Father, who raised him from the dead) . . ."

The apostle Paul, among other things, had received his education under Gamaliel. In fact, prior to conversion, his name was Saul. He was born in Tarsus in a place called Cilicia, which is now modern-day Turkey. Among other things, he was a master contractor and a builder of tents by profession. Prior to his Damascus Road experience, he was a man of brutality and violence, a persecutor of the church.

Through his conversion experience on Damascus Road, Paul was transformed into the apostle of grace. He became a church founder, and as so, like all apostles, had authority over the churches that he or they founded. Paul and Barnabas "ordained them elders in every church, and prayed with fasting, and commended them to the Lord, on whom they believed" (Acts 14:23). Paul also appointed Titus to ordain Elders and set the church in order at Crete (Titus 1:5), as stated, *"How shall they call on him in whom they have not believed' 'and, how shall they hear without a preacher?' 'And how shall they preach except they are sent?'"* (Rom. 10:14–15)

If you are called by God and walk in one of the previously mentioned Mantles of Ministry gifts, you must know that you are authorized by the Word of God as a chosen vessel of Christ to bear and carry His Name before the world; to help people; to bring forth His people, the people of God; to bring forth good fruit, works associated with kingdom building and spiritual growth; and to confound the wise and mighty.

You are commissioned to stand as a minister and witness of all you have experienced and to compel humankind to repent from evil and to amend their ways, to encourage them to forsake other gods and turn to the true and living God, to listen to Him, and to become an ambassador for Christ.

You are authorized to urge people to be reconciled to God, to go forth; to stand and speak the words of life; to preach the Word, reprove, rebuke, exhort, and teach; to baptize; to open people's eyes and turn them from darkness to light, and from Satan to God; to get them to repent and be forgiven; and to declare God's glory and wonders. In addition, each of the Five-Fold Ministry Gifts or Mantles of Ministry are coupled with the gift of teaching. Without the ability to teach as well as preach or prophecy we are ineffective in our delivery to others.

The Mantle Of Apostle-Teacher

Ephesians 2:20–22 (KJV):

> *"And are built upon the foundation of the apostles and prophets, Jesus Christ himself being the chief cornerstone; In whom all the building fitly framed together groweth unto a holy temple in the Lord: In whom ye also are built together for a habitation of God through the Spirit."*

The following offices describe the positions and functions of the ascension gifts. The above scriptures, Ephesians 4:10–13 and 2:20, inform us that no one's place or role in these ascension gifts are higher than the giver of these gifts. Jesus Christ, our Lord, is head of all things. We reverence him alone, yet, we respect everyone. He has invested in the Mantle of Ministry gifts placed upon us. He has placed these things in position in the body of Christ for our good, well-being, growth, and maturity, and that we might be complete in Him.

It is in the Book of Acts 26: 16–18 that the mandate call of the apostle is clearly stated. Paul who had been an accuser of the brethren, a persecutor of the church, is now divinely approached by Jesus Christ the Son of the living God, who after knocking Paul from his ride, informs him in what we recognize as the divine call and purpose of the apostle: *Rise* and *stand* on your feet. I have appeared to you to tell you who you are and what you will receive from me to:

- make you a minister and a witness unto me
- tell you of the power and authority you have and will receive from me
- do my work

- proclaim Me to people who know me and those who do not
- open their eyes
- turn them from darkness and to bring them into the light
- turn them from the power of Satan, and
- bring them to their God
- receive forgiveness
- receive the inheritance of those sanctified by the faith that only comes from me.

Acts 26:16–18

> But rise, and stand upon thy feet: for I have appeared unto thee for this purpose, to make thee a minister and a witness both of these things which thou hast seen, and of those things in the which I will appear unto thee; delivering thee from the people, and from the Gentiles, unto whom now I send thee, to open their eyes, and to turn them from darkness to light, and from the power of Satan unto God, that they may receive forgiveness of sins, and inheritance among them which are sanctified by faith that is in me.

It is a fact that the apostles were given, in one significant aspect, as a fundamental part of the foundation of the church, Christ's temple. Many believe that the dispensation of the apostle has passed and that they only served in the preliminary stages of the first-century church. So, many think that the work or original assignment of the apostle was completed by the first twelve apostles in the New Testament dispensation and that this gift no longer functions, and therefore, no longer play a role of the direction of the church.

As we have come to understand and to know, the word *apostle* in Greek implies the sent ones are those sent out for a specific purpose. We have further learned that this purpose could mean that this individual's function could be assigned to implement other or new work, such as ministries or churches, or could be a bearer of a specific or divine message.

Being guided with this frame of thought, one can see the significances of the functioning gift of apostle even in this dispensation of the church hour. God is still calling men and women to the forefront of ministry, those with specific work to implement, and or a divine message to be delivered. These men and women have the formidable task of breaking through barriers, faulty thinking; ideology; or more distinctly, spiritual strongholds in individuals' lives; geographical locations; and so on. To be more specific, as messengers, the apostle are implementers or advocates on behalf of the Father for His church. They are sent forth:

- to up-build kingdom ministry here on earth,
- as a supporter of specific programs and ministry services and
- as promoters of God's work eternally as they embrace all areas of ministry.

Not All Apostles Are the Same

No one can measure whether an apostle's fit or extent of the length of their calling based on the work of another. Not all apostles are alike in function because they are not all called to do the same thing. Therefore, they may vary in their degree or level of operation based on the grace given them for their specific assignment. They may even appear to have one focused message, which is because of the task given to that individual. However, all apostles have the kingdom authority to both authorize and implement whatever they have been anointed, appointed, and assigned to do.

There is unique gifting on the life of the apostle. The apostle is one explicitly called out and sent forth to solve or resolve issues that need special attention and strategies. The apostle has an extraordinary and sometimes exceptional revelation of situations and the ability to teach awareness that leads to resolution. Often this form or method of teaching and preaching may relate to one unambiguous message or area, such as deliverance from spiritual and physical bondage, financial breakthrough, or correct perception of an issue.

The apostle presents with strong dynamic encouragement that will guide individuals from becoming a future prey of any potential spiritual impediment or hindrance. The apostle Paul was such an example. Let us look at his credentials through the lens of Scripture "whereunto I have ordained a preacher, and an apostle (I speak the truth in Christ, and lie not), a teacher of the Gentiles in faith and verity" (1 Tim. 2:7, KJV). Thus, Paul was the preacher, the apostle, and the teacher

The Mantle Of Prophet-Teacher

The role of the prophet, like that of the elder, has transcended time throughout scripture, even until today. The elder and prophet are both mentioned in the Book of Revelation. A prophet of the Lord is one whose gift is to help in guiding the people of God into all truths. The Old Testament often referred to them as seers.

The prophet also is given in one significant aspect as a fundamental part of the foundation of the church, Christ's temple. The gift of the prophet of the five-fold gifts, Mantles of Ministry, functions in foretelling of the future. The prophet is, therefore, assigned to the populace where there is a place and purpose for vision. The message that the prophet usually brings is that of correction. They speak the Word of the Lord, as they function in ministry as his eyes, ears, and mouthpiece. There is no gender dominance concerning this gift. Both the Old and the New Testaments speak of men and women who exercised in the gift of prophecy, many of which were working-class people. Some examples from the Old Testament include:

- Moses was of the Levite priesthood by heredity. He was also raised as a Prince of Egypt by adoption. While running from Egypt after killing an Egyptian for harming a Hebrew, he became a shepherd in the hills of Midian. He later had an encounter with God that caused him to return to Egypt to free the Hebrews; he became their deliverer, prophet, and king.
- Miriam, called the prophetess, served alongside Moses and their brother Aaron, and the three of them became known as the delivers who brought the Hebrews out of Egypt.
- Deborah ("bee") was a leader. When the nation of Israel seemed crushed, and without hope, evil prevailed in the land. She then raised, Deborah as a mother, prophet, and judge

- adjudicating the matters of the Israelites. She was pivotal in directing the course of Israel and for bringing deliverance once again to God's chosen people.
- Samuel served Israel during its darkest era as a Levite priest, a prophet, and a judge. Samuel was one of the greatest of God's prophets to the nation Israel.
- Jeremiah was sanctified as a prophet to the nation while in his mother's womb. He lived a life of celibacy and remained faithful amid hardship and ridicule, even to the point of feeling like giving up, but he prevailed, saying Jehovah's Words were like fire shut up in his bones.
- Nathan-served as a prophet to the kings during the reigns of David and Solomon, when David violated Uriah the Hittite by taking his wife Bathsheba, and then losing his life on the king's orders. Nathan was assigned the task to reprove King David for these actions (2 Sam. 12:1–14).
- Huldah served in the capacity as a university teacher in Jerusalem. It was during the reign of King Josiah that focus was drawn to this remarkable woman of God. She served as prophetess during the same time in Biblical history as Zephaniah and Jeremiah. However, rather than seeking counsel from either of the two concerning an urgent matter, the King sought counsel from Huldah.
- Amos was not a major prophet, nor did he descend through the line of prophets. Amos by profession tended herds and dressed sycamore trees. Amos came to prominence as a minor prophet during the reign of King Uzziah of Judah.

There were many others, including Ezra, Daniel, Nehemiah, Elijah and Elisha, Joel, Jonah, and Ezekiel. Some examples of those engaging in prophetic ministry in the New Testament include:

- Jesus Christ Himself
- John the Baptist
- The four virgin daughters of the evangelist Philip. Philip was also one of the seven men chosen to serve (Acts 21:9).

- Judas, surnamed Barnabas, and Silas were also called Silvanus (Acts 15:32).

Remember, prophecy is a gift to the body, and God utilizes whom He choose. However, not everyone who prophesies has the ministry of a prophet. As spoken, "And afterward, I will pour out my Spirit upon all flesh, and your sons and daughters shall prophecy" (Joel 2:28; Acts 2:17).

The word *prophet* comes from the Hebrew word "*nabi*" meaning to "bubble forth, as from a fountain. Prophecy is the ability to foretell or, more accurately, to forthtell. In this dispensation of the church, the purpose of this gift's function is more often to exhort, edify, encourage, bring correction/rebuke, and to strengthen believers in Christ. As the minister, the prophet:

- **Exhorts**—by recommending and helping to set in motion of a person's direction to Jesus through building the individual's confidence to become adamant and to persevere as he or she takes or progress in their walk of faith in the Lord.
- **Edifies**—by advocating and encouraging as in urging others by offering strong advice to individuals as they move forward in the Lord, and the plan and the will of God for their lives.
- **Comforts**—by reassuring, and or restoring confidence, and by consoling and raising the spirit of the individuals they to minister too as well as
- Correction/rebuke—is all-inclusive in the above.

Deuteronomy 18:18–19 (KJV)

I will raise them a Prophet from among their brethren, like unto thee, and will put my words in his mouth; and he shall speak unto them all that I shall command him. And it shall come to pass, that whosoever will not hearken unto my words which he shall speak in my name, I will require it of him.

1 Corinthians 12:28 (KJV)

"And God hath set some in the church, first apostles, secondarily prophets, thirdly teachers, after that miracles, then gifts of healings, helps, governments, diversities of tongues."

Numbers 12:6, 8 (KJV)

And he said, Hear now my words: If there be a prophet among you, I the Lord will make myself known unto him in a vision, and will speak unto him in a dream. With him will I speak mouth to mouth, even apparently, and not in dark speeches; and the similitude of the Lord shall he behold: wherefore then were ye not afraid to speak against my servant Moses?

Isaiah 51:16 (KJV)

And I have put my words in thy mouth, and I have covered thee in the shadow of mine hand, that I may plant the heavens, and lay the foundations of the earth, and say unto Zion, Thou art my people.

2 Peter 1:20–21 (KJV)

Knowing this first, that no prophecy of the scripture is of any private interpretation. [21] For the prophecy came not in old time by the will of man: but holy men of God spake as the Holy Ghost moved them.

Ephesians 3:5 (KJV)

Which in other ages was not made known unto the sons of men, as it is now revealed unto his holy apostles and prophets by the Spirit.

The Mantle Of Evangelist-Teacher

The evangelist is to proclaim the gospel of Good News, designed to loosen humankind from spiritual bondage and sin, offering hope in despair and drawing the hopeless and downtrodden to the saving knowledge of Christ. We will bring our focus to three areas that deeply relate to those who walk under the Mantle of the Evangelist, which include:

- The image of the evangelist
- The integrity of the evangelist and the
- The work of the evangelist

Paul instructed his son in ministry to "do the work of an evangelist." The work of the evangelist is to spread the good news of the gospel. Every born-again believer in Christ is to function in this capacity at one time or another. However, some walk in this mandate called "evangelist." As such, one must take this appointment seriously and hold it in the highest esteem, with their reputation guarded against being tarnished with an evil report.

The Mantle Of Pastor—Teacher

As stated in scripture, "And I will give you pastors according to mine heart, which shall feed you with knowledge and understanding" (Jer. 3:15 KJV). Also, Jeremiah stated in 17:16, "As for me, I have not hastened from being a pastor to follow thee: neither have I desired the woeful day; thou knowest: that which came out of my lips was right before thee."

The mantle of pastor is a spiritual gift to the church. According to New Testament teachings, we see this gift from three perspectives: (1) Poimen (2) Pesbuteros, and (3) Episkopeo. Therefore, from the perspective of Poimen, the pastor is the shepherd of the flock. As a shepherd, he or she is a helper and a nurturer of the people of God. These individuals are appointed or set in the church over the congregation. The word pastor describes one who serves. These individuals are an ordained elder or reverend of the Christian church. He or she is to teach, lead, guide, and protect the (sheep) people of God in all areas that pertain to life and well-being.

This includes the five aspects concerning humankind:

- Spiritual: John 3:3, 11; 2 Corinthians 5:17–21; Romans 10:9–10
- Mental: 2 Timothy 1:7; Romans 12:2; Isaiah 26:3
- Physical: Isaiah 53:4–5; Matthew 8:17; 1 Peter 2:24
- Financial: 3 John 2; Malachi 3:10–11; Luke 6:38; 2 Corinthians 9:6–10; Deuteronomy 28:1–14
- Social: Proverbs 3:4

Also, from the perspective of *episkopeo*, pastors are referred to as overseers of the flock. Therefore, as overseers, they are instructed to "shepherd the flock of God which is among you, serving as overseers, not by constraint but willingly, not for dishonest gain but eagerly; nor as being lords over those entrusted to you, but being examples to the flock" (1 Pet. 5:2–3).

In serving as a senior pastor or shepherd, the responsibilities are many and diverse. This gift is closely related to the spiritual gifts of leadership and teaching and means shepherd or overseer. In the Biblical context, shepherds had several different responsibilities to their sheep and, ultimately, to the owner of the sheep. They kept a lookout for predators and protected the sheep from attackers. They cared for wounded and sick sheep, nursing them back to health. They rescued them if they became lost or trapped.

The shepherd spent enormous amounts of time with the sheep, guiding them to the places of nourishment and rest. The result was a trust and relationship that kept the sheep following the shepherd. The sheep knew their shepherd's voice to the point that even if they temporarily mixed with another herd, at the call of the shepherd, they would separate and follow him.

Pastors are called shepherds because their calling and gifting are much like those who care for sheep. They are called and gifted to care for the spiritual well-being of a local body of God's people. Pastors are first and foremost servants. They are servants of God and servants of His bride, the church. They are given a mixture of abilities by grace that allows them to serve the needs of an entire community.

The goal of the pastor is to teach the truth about God and the power of the Holy Spirit. The primary way the pastor will do this is by explaining the Word of God to the church. Therefore, the gift of pastor links to that of teaching in Ephesians 4:11 and elsewhere. This gift could be called the gift of pastor-teacher. The ability to teach the Scriptures is also one of the many requirements of being an overseer (1 Tim. 3:1–7; Titus 1:6–9). By explaining the Scriptures to the church, the pastor feeds the "sheep" of God.

The Holy Spirit gives the spiritual gift of the pastor to some in the church to humbly teach them, guide them, protect them, and to lead them in the mission that God has for His church, namely the Great

Commission. The pastor loves the Gospel of Jesus Christ and puts it at the center of his life and ministry. Pastors do not seek fame or recognition for themselves; however, they in a position of authority by the Holy Spirit. The role of a pastor is one of humility and service as he is reminded daily of his overwhelming need of God's grace for the task at hand. See also Ephesians 4:11; Jeremiah 3:15; Acts 20:28; John 10:11–18.

The apostle Paul wrote some of the qualifications of a pastor. "For a bishop must be blameless, as a steward of God, not self-willed, not quick-tempered, not given to wine, not violent, not greedy for money, but hospitable, a lover of what is right, sober-minded, just, holy, self-controlled, holding fast the faithful word as he has been taught, that he may be able, by sound doctrine, both to exhort and convict those who contradict" (Titus 1:7–9). Simply put, a pastor is to minister to the needs of a group of believers.

The senior pastor shall serve as the chief under-shepherd and overseer of this local church, feeding, leading, and nurturing the sheep. This person's primary responsibilities will be to:

1. Communicate God's Word, minister to spiritual needs, and provide biblical leadership for the church.
2. Provide leadership and vision for the church, direct plans for ministry and church growth, develop and fine-tune the church structure based on the team philosophy of ministry.
3. Motivate, equip, and nurture the people of the church through example, preaching and teaching God's Word and spiritual counseling.
4. Spend considerable time in prayer and Bible study.
5. Contact/visit hospitalized or grieving church members.
6. Officiate at weddings and funerals.
7. Provide premarital counseling, counseling regarding salvation and spiritual issues, and other advice for church members as time permits.
8. Perform sacraments such as Communion and baptism.
9. Oversee church discipline and manage conflict in the church. Seek to reconcile relationships and promote unity within the church.

10. Participate in evangelism efforts through preaching and giving invitations during worship services, revival, or other special services, visitation, and other outreach efforts.

A shepherding ministry does not merely feed but in other aspects help care for the flock and is used metaphorically of Christian pastors. Responsibilities that appear connected with pastoral ministry include oversight and care of the saints, providing spiritual food for their growth and development, leadership, guidance, and counsel. The title was usually given to the senior minister of the local church, regardless of his or her five-fold calling. Their leadership role can and may often extend to elders, overseers, bishops, etc. Prophetic pastors not only do the things usually associated with pastoring but also move with supernatural graces and gifting of God such as prophesying, having a word of knowledge, healing, and have the vision and willingness to develop the saints in their gifts and callings.

Section 3

We Are Examples Of God's Grace And Mercy!

That is why we walk by faith and not by sight and as we grow more in His grace and love, we become better examples of expressing His happiness that flows through our hearts daily.

- **Faith** is one of the necessities of pleasing God, for without it is impossible to please Him. Most importantly, we are the family of God and Jehovah God almighty is our Father.
- **Growing** in God's grace, we are very cheerful givers to those who are in need. We are kind, gentle, and true glorifiers of God.

Happiness has filled our hearts since we met the Savior. We have the Spirit's gift of hope and humility. We are delivered from sickness because God has sent forth His word to heal us. His Holy Ghost guides us while we travel on to a heavenly home (Wooden, 1983).

The Overseer And Bishop

Overseer is another word that transcends both the Old and New Testament. The Hebrew word *overseer* (*paqivd—pa-ked*) or (*shoter—sho-tar*), as seen in the Old Testament, means an officer, an official representative, an executive, one who governs or is an administrator. The word *overseer* (*episkopos or e-pe-sko-pos*), as seen in the New Testament, Greek translation, means *bishop*.

From a religious perspective, the word overseer implies one having the oversight of positions, people, and of church and administrative affairs. No one governing body has jurisdiction over another on how these offices work. The structure, format, and executive administration are designed explicitly as a best fit for the organization or fellowship to which these officers serve.

In many organizations or fellowships, the overseer is the highest level of the chain of command. The structure is not to be a dispute because of another's belief. Their belief may honestly be based on their perspective of organizational structure, especially if they have concluded that scripture views both overseer and the bishop as having a similar meaning. Always remember and respect the fact that some things are structured based on how various individuals may understand or interpret a translation.

The Bishop

A *bishop* (*episkopos* or *episcopos*), as described in the New Testament Hebrew translation, is someone who oversees and directs the functioning and proper operations of a church or churches under his or her care. As we can see in Acts 20:17–28; 1 Peter 5:1–2; Philippians 1:1;

and 1 Timothy 3, during apostolic times, there was no specific distinction between an elder, overseer and a bishop.

However, as the church developed into a more structured work of ministry, the offices of elder, overseer, and bishop became more defined, although in many ways, the latter two (overseer and bishop) are synonymous in meaning. Both are now assigned more distinct duties and responsibilities. Jesus is Chief in charge. He alone is our Chief overseer and is "the bishop of our souls" (1 Pet. 2:25).

Because of hardship and tribulations endured during the first-century church, the office of a bishop was a commendable desire to have. Those who qualified for such a position were required to live exceptionable extraordinary lives and were presented as an exceptional role model in the church, which Jesus paid for with His blood. These individuals were required to live a life of integrity and dignity, which appertain to the office.

Some have asked, where do the elder, overseer, and bishop fit into the five-fold ministry gifts of Ephesians 4:11—"And he gave some, apostles; and some, prophets; and some, evangelists; and some, pastors and teachers." Well, the answer to that question is they fit perfectly into this God-given equation. God has a purpose and a plan for all things, and He never wastes anything.

These three distinctions so intimately spring from the office of pastor. The pastor may appear to be toward the bottom of the five-fold ministry gifts. However, it happens to be one of, if not, the most significant functions of ministry. He or she continuously bears the task of caring, feeding, and protecting those in their care. Jesus asked Peter, "loveth thou me?" His instructions then and now are to "feed my sheep." The pastor feeds pray, and cares for the needs of the sheep continuously.

QUALIFICATIONS OF BISHOPS

1 Timothy 3 and **Acts 20:28 (KJV)**
"Take heed therefore unto yourselves, and to all the flock, over the which the Holy Ghost hath made you overseers, to feed the church of God, which he hath purchased with his blood. **Hebrews 13:7 (KJV)**

"Remember them which have the rule over you, who have spoken unto you the word of God: whose faith follow, considering the end of their conversation."

1 Thessalonians 5:12 (KJV)
And we beseech you, brethren, to know them which labor among you, and are over you in the Lord, and admonish you.

The Purpose of License and Ordination

All born-again believers have a call to minister to the lost. They are called to pray for the sick, feed the hungry, and so on. Therefore, no one needs to be licensed or ordained to do so. However, for those engaging in full-time ministry, there are proper credentials that include licensing and ordination from a recognized body of believers in Christ. For the individual who holds either of these credentials, they are privileged with having three distinct statements of acknowledgment, which are:

- The acceptance of the call of God on a worker's life.
- Your spiritual leader acknowledges this call and, therefore, has licensed or ordained you to the position.
- It states to the world that you are a qualified worker.
- Thus, your credentials will open doors for you, allowing you access to various places you could not have gone otherwise.

There are many questions concerning the rights of a licensed minister performing a wedding. In most states, it is a criminal offense punishable by a small fine or short prison sentence for one to perform a marriage ceremony if they are not authorized to do so by state law. In most states, a minister has the authority to perform marriages. Some states require a minister to be licensed, or ordained, while others expect them to be licensed and appointed. To determine the requirements of your state, merely make a phone call to your state's marriage license bureau and ask them.

Each state that makes up the United States of America has legal codes pertaining to who can and cannot perform weddings. Any licensed minister should check its state requirements prior to accepting such a responsibility. In some states, ministers can obtain their credential via online application; however, on the other hand, some states do not accept online credentials. For instance, guidelines for a minister to perform weddings in the State of Virginia, they must produce before the judge or clerk of the Circuit Court of any County or City Court proof of their:

- Licensing or ordination and of their being in regular communion with their religious society or denomination.
- Alternately, proof that they hold a local minister's license, and are serving as a pastor or leader of a local church or sect.

I reiterate—ordination and regular communion with religious society/denomination, or proof of minister's license if serving as a pastor or leader of a local church or sect are in many cases required.

THE LICENSED MINISTERS

It is important to know that the word *minister* transcends the time and language of both the Old and New Testaments of the Bible. As seen in the Hebrew and Aramaic translations, the word minister (*Pel-akh'* or *pelah*) refers to a religious class of sanctuary servants, as seen in Ezra 2:55–58, 7:24 and Nehemiah 7:57–60. In the New Testament Greek, the word minister (*diakonia* or *diaconos*) refers to an assistant or subordinate officer engaged in ministry, which include Christ our Lord, Paul and Apollos, Epaphras, Timothy, and Tychicu as seen in the following passages of scripture:

- ✓ Romans 15:8
- ✓ 1Colossians 3:5
- ✓ Colossians 1:7
- ✓ 1Thessalonian 3:2 and
- ✓ Ephesians 6:21

Thus, the word minister means to serve.

Mistakenly many have confused the role of the minister, licensed minister, and the ordained elder. The minister and licensed minister, although similar, do not function on the same level of that of an ordained elder. However, in most situations, becoming a minister is entry-level. Next is the ordained elder or reverend in the ministry of the church.

The scripture instructs us not to place a novice in certain positions of leadership, such as that of the ordained elder's or reverend position. There are specific levels of training that help toward qualifying an individual for each position. Remember, individuals engaging in ministry are perceived by their life's character, as displayed in the attributes of the fruit of the Spirit.

1 Thessalonians 5:12–13 KJV

> "And we beseech you, brethren, to know them which labor among you, and are over you in the Lord, and admonish you; And to esteem them very highly in love for their work's sake. And be at peace among yourselves."

Therefore, before being elevated to the office of elder, these individuals must apply themselves to the discipline of the grace of God to the position, and to the study of the Word, as stated in 2 Timothy 2:15: "study to show thyself approved unto God a workman that needeth not to be ashamed, rightly dividing the word of truth."

The minister serves in the capacity of the disciple, as one in training. The ordained elder is someone who has more experience in ministry. In other words, the elder has come up through the ranks of training and has met all requirements of a qualified good steward of the Gospel and to spiritual maturity. With this, ministers, therefore, must go through various training and classes for leadership development that includes specialized training, which could consist of:

- Extra-curricular studies from a religious institution approved of by their leader, in-house training, and instructions as designed and or presented by their pastor(s). The minister in training (MIT) is a part of the ministerial staff of a church, and their ministry will eventually lead to:

- Participating in and conducting religious services.

Ministers, in some settings, are ambassadors. An ambassador is someone commissioned as a representative of church affairs.

- A minister is someone who takes care of those assigned to him or her.

Licensed ministers, in some cases, become pastors before being ordained to the position of an elder.

- A minister is one called to serve and is apt to teach and or preach.
- A minister who performs weddings in some states can do so but must have an official clergy member sign the legal document. In such cases, a minister cannot sign the marriage certificate because he or she is not an ordained clergy member and is therefore not authorized by his or her church and state of residence to do so. (Please refer to the area addressing performing weddings.
- A minister can perform a eulogy at a funeral if requested or approved by a family to do so.

Section 4
WE ARE THE LIGHTS BY WHICH OTHERS FIND GOD!

Lifted from the depths of sin by the power of God's outstretched hands, we have become more concerned for all mankind. We have become lights to the blind as we walk in the likeness of Christ, for God's love continually fills our hearts.

Meditation is a daily part of our lives. By making this a regular routine, we can be more effective witnesses of God's miraculous miracle working power. Also, our minds are set toward being the true missionaries God expects us to be in our earthly ministry.

Notwithstanding, we reside in this land. Thus, we are natives of the kingdom of God. As we hold onto the Savior's hand, we experience the new birth through the regeneration of the Holy Ghost (Wooden, 1983).

The Elders

The word *elder* sometimes refers to someone older, male, or female. However, in relation to the church and the work of the ministry, the word elder has a significant purpose. An elder is not based on the age of an individual, but rather on the individual's maturity in God. This maturity comes through the unction and anointing of the Holy Spirit upon and within the life of a faithful spirit-filled believer in Christ.

In respect to a multiplicity of terminology among denominations or organizations in Christian settings, the title elder may differ. It remains prevalent that the role of elders has always been significant in the lives of God's people and the church and has transcended time from the Old Testament through the New Testament and even unto today. In most settings, the word refers to someone engaged in ministry, such as a clergy member.

In His infinite wisdom and plan for the church, God has always utilized the: wisdom, knowledge, oversight, counsel, conflict resolution, decision making, and leadership skills and abilities of eldership.

The office of elder is the highest ordained position in the local church besides that of the pastor, which is an ordained elder or reverend. However, this does not include the office of overseer or a bishop. The office of overseer is an elevated position, and the office of bishop is a consecrated position. In many church settings, this is a board. The board is made up of qualified men and women who have met both spiritual and moral requirements. These are individuals who have acknowledged the call of God upon his or her life. It is this group that composes the presbytery of the church.

A candidate for elder cannot be a novice, which means inexperienced. He or she must be one who has come up through the ranks of the ministry. He or she must be found worthy by their pastor, because of their stewardship toward the gospel and the affairs of the church. The ordained elder in the most Christian churches functions as the guardian of the doctrine of God and His church, and they serve in many capacities to include:

- Deliverers of the Word,
- Those without charge (serving under leadership within their local church) or
- Those serving as pastors of a local congregation.

The elders are in place to help bear the weight of the ministry. Whenever mentioned in scripture, the word elder appears in a plural context, signifying the significance of the role of elders as a group rather than a single individual. Although for church order there is a hierarchical approach in ministry, the plurality of the word elders emphasizes that the work of the Lord neither is nor ever was intended to function by a single person. Eldership is a shared office within the body, and these individuals serve as shepherds or under-shepherds of the flock, the people of God. Remember, we are workers together with Him.

God never intended for any one person to take the full weight of His people or His church. We see this in the case with Moses in Numbers 11:6 and 17, as God was establishing His nation and people. This statement is not meant to diminish the importance of church order. There is an order to things, and we will discuss that subject in more length in an upcoming section that bears that title.

Numbers 11:16–17 (KJV)

> *"And the Lord said unto Moses, Gather unto me seventy men of the elders of Israel, whom thou knowest to be the elders of the people, and officers over them; and bring them unto the tabernacle of the congregation, that they may stand there with thee. And I will come down and talk with thee there: and I will take of the spirit which is upon thee, and will put it upon them; and they shall bear the burden of the people with thee, that thou bear it not thyself alone.*

The Qualifications of the Elder, Overseer, and Bishop

Titus 1:5–9 (KJV)
For this cause left I thee in Crete, that thou shouldest set in order the things that are wanting, and ordain elders in every city, as I had appointed thee: If any be blameless, (author wants list in 2 columns)

- *The husband of one wife,*
- *Having faithful children not accused of riot or unruly.*
- *For a bishop must be blameless, as the steward of God.*
- *Not self-willed,*
- *Not soon angry,*
- *Not given to wine,*
- *No striker,*
- *Not given to filthy lucre.*
- *But a lover of hospitality,*
- *A lover of good men,*
- *Sober,*
- *Just,*
- *Holy,*
- *Temperate.*
- *Holding fast the faithful word as he hath been taught that he may be able by sound doctrine both to exhort and to convince the gainsayers.*

The Charge To The Elder

1 Peter 5:1–4 (KJV).

> *"The elders which are among you I exhort, who am also an elder, and a witness of the sufferings of Christ, and also a partaker of the glory that shall be revealed: Feed the flock of God which is among you, taking the oversight thereof, not by constraint, but willingly; not for filthy lucre, but of a ready mind; Neither as being lords over God's heritage, but being ensamples to the flock. And when the chief Shepherd shall appear, ye shall receive a crown of glory that fadeth not away."*

The Ordained Elder Charged To:

- The Word of God
- The sacraments and the orders of the church
- The oversight and care of the flock of God

A Two-Part Commitment And Crowning Reward Of Honor

A lifetime commitment on the part of the candidate, as well as a lifetime appointment from God, are what is required of an elder. All that you have endured to this point was all in preparation for this position. An elder has charge, overseers, and bishops. The word elder can also imply senior as in senior pastor or leader as in Christian leader and is also synonymous to the word's overseer and bishop. Each of these words refers to the pastors of the New Testament church.

1 Peter 5:1–2 (KJV)

> *The elders which are among you I exhort, who am also an elder, and a witness of the sufferings of Christ, and even a partaker of the glory that shall be revealed: 2 Feed the flock of God which is among you, taking the oversight thereof, not by constraint, but willingly; not for filthy lucre, but of a ready mind;*

Within The Local Assembly

The Role of the Missionary

I previously work a self-published workbook, *NUGGETS*, for women engaging in ministry. That book emphasized on the overall view of the missionary, which included every level that consists of the area of women working in ministry. However, my understanding of the call to ministry, specifically, *The Mantle of Ministry, Embracing the Call*, perspective has broadened. So, on behalf of those women engaging in ministry (WEIM) as missionaries, I now write.

A missionary is a propagator. A propagator is someone who broadcasts, proliferates, circulates, publicizes, spreads the news, or plants. The missionary's job in this capacity is to:

- ✓ Convert others to the saving knowledge of Jesus Christ as Lord.
- ✓ Be sent on a mission.
- ✓ Proclaims the Good News of the Gospel. However, this proclamation does not have to take place within a church setting. The harvest is plenteous, but the laborers are few.
- ✓ Focus on the promotion of economic development, literacy, education, health care and orphanages, all within her local church setting and perhaps the world.

A WEIM does not seek to be pulpit centered, but her focus and main concern is about helping to meet the needs of people; she is soul-winning centered. She realizes that the whole world around her is her pulpit and that the soul in need that she meets is her audience.

Therefore, the aim of every member of the board of WEIM should be to lead people to express their Christian discipleship in every area of human life and to help ensure that the kingdom of God is realized. There are various areas of women's ministry in the local church, including: the Mantle of Ministry offices, which include the apostle, prophet, evangelist, pastor, and teacher as well as the *offices of command: the bishop, overseer and elder, minister, the licensed missionary, and aspiring missionary.*

We will now focus on the aspiring missionary and the licensed missionary. A missionary in the local assembly is one who feels a strong call of God upon her life to work in the ministry of the church. Her response of yes to God's desire for her life becomes an eternal yielding and surrender. Her aim is to draw close to God and into the center of His will, as she encourages others to an awareness and commitment to Him. *Missionary* means, disciple, follower, and messenger. From these descriptions, you can see that there are three specific areas addressed, which are:

- ✓ The area of training,
- ✓ The area of submitting to and to be led, and
- ✓ The area of being a courier, envoy, or a herald

The Aspiring Missionary

Because of the various areas of becoming equipped, the first level of WEIM is the aspiring missionary. The implementation of this level consists of biblical instruction to prevent placing a novice in leadership position. In other words, this is an entry level into ministry work in the local church. The title derives from the idea of one aspiring to become and who is willing to go through the process required to being who the individual aspires to be.

Usually, in many church settings the aspiring missionary is a young woman of legal age, who has presented herself in good Christian standard, and who walks in alignment and allegiance with leadership. She strongly feels a special call of God on her life. Her life must be that of a godly example. She must be concerned about her church. She must be a woman of prayer and a strong believer in the study and application of the Word of God. She must be a woman capable of teaching the word and have a love for soul-winning, as well as one who feels the inner call to the service of God.

A woman entering this phase of the ministry must be observed for a specific time frame, which in many settings is a length of at least two years under the watchful eye of her pastor. In that time, she will be required to attend workshops and other training classes recommended by her leader before moving into the next position, which is that of the licensed missionary.

OTHER CRITERIA:

- ✓ An aspiring missionary should confess to salvation, sanctification, and filled with the Holy Ghost.
- ✓ She must first prove herself faithful, one who practices self-control and possesses a good moral standard of conduct.
- ✓ She must be one who studies to show soundness herself approved unto God rightly dividing the word of truth.
- ✓ She must have a true concern for God's people, encouraging those who are a part of her local church as well as anyone that she may meet. She should always practice brotherly love. Read Hebrew 12:1.
- ✓ She must be active in the work of the church, in prayer, and capable to teach. "Whatever, your hands find to do, do it as unto the Lord" (Eccl. 9:10, KJV). Just let what you are doing be done in decency and in order, and with the blessings of your pastor.
- ✓ She must be actively involved in the soul-winning ministry of her church.
- ✓ She must be knowledgeable of the doctrine of her church, the church's mission, and its protocol.
- ✓ She must attend and participate on Sunday/church school, Bible study, pastoral services, and regularly scheduled services.
- ✓ She must know what appropriate dress attire is for specific occasions.

Her specific duties are within the confines of her local church. However, if she receives an invitation to serve outside the confines of her local church, she may do so with the permission of her pastor, but her church mother or a licensed missionary, or someone else of position in her local ministry must accompany her.

Upon the completion of observation by her pastor, and proper training, the aspiring missionary will then be examined by her pastor, the supervisor of the WEIM and/or the board of examiners. In many established church dominations, the board of examiners is made up of the supervisor or in some places she is known as the president of WEIM and a group of licensed missionaries that are selected by the apostle, bishop, overseer, or pastor. If she passes the examination, she will then become a licensed missionary.

The Licensed Missionary

A licensed missionary is one who has gone through all the phases of an aspiring missionary and has served well in this capacity. Her life should be that of a woman of God who has applied herself to the study of the Word of God as her rule of faith and practice, seeking knowledge from God and training through Bible school, institute classes, and so on. This will better equip her to serve God and His people knowledgeably.

Her purpose is to serve her local church and to help build the work of God in the women's department, which will enhance the general work. The licensed missionary, as recommended, however, is not necessarily the norm. After two years of in-service training, if led by God, her activities could lead to the evangelist ministry.

The Transition from Licensed Missionary to Evangelist

There are still many church bodies where the evangelist missionary is one who has successfully gone through the phases of an aspiring missionary and a licensed missionary, and whose ministry extends outside the local church assembly into other church settings upon invitation as a speaker. It is important to note here, that not all evangelist missionaries have outside speaking engagements. However, to fill any outside speaking engagements, she must have the endorsement of her pastor. She is expected to help build the work of her local church on all levels.

Also, she must be available to travel, and conduct revivals wherever or whenever called upon. Her in-house motivation should be directed to education, through implementing workshops and seminars for developing other women to care for and to love their church and leaders.

Section 5

WE ARE COMMITTED AND REWARDED FOR OUR FAITHFULNESS TO GOD!

Obligated to teach observance of all things commanded to us by Christ, we know that obedience is better than sacrifice. By so doing these things we become one with God the Father, God the Son and God the Holy Ghost.

Precious in God's sight, we are filled with His peace, which passes all understanding. We are pilgrims on our way to paradise, striving every day toward perfection. Being empowered with the Holy Ghost, we have received power over spiritual wickedness in high places, including demoniac spirits and Satan.

Quickened through the Holy Spirit, we have become revived in our hearts, souls, and minds. We have been qualified by God for the witnessing of His word to the sinner man (Wooden, 1983).

Recognizing The Call

So, you say you are called. Well, how do you know?
As stated by Peter, "Wherefore the rather, brethren, give diligence to make your calling and election sure: for if ye do these things, ye shall never fall: For so an entrance shall be ministered unto you abundantly into the everlasting kingdom of our Lord and Savior Jesus Christ" (2 Peter 1:10–11 KJV).

Regardless to whoever we are, our gender, ethnicity, or position in life, those experiencing the call to ministry, will individually face the challenge of answering these questions: how do you know that you are called, what is your calling, and how do you go about responding to your call to ministry? Recognizing God's voice and His call will always be challenging. The reason is the enemy never intends for anyone of us to give ourselves willingly to and for the Master's use.

Therefore, the enemy, confronts us with many different situations in life, which are intended to make us become faint at heart, to draw back in faith and spirit, and even to retreat to prevent us from ever engaging in ministry. In other words, when there is a definite calling on an individual's life, they will tend to struggle with the mere thought of answering that call and of seeing themselves worthy of such a call, especially that of entering the ministry.

The Fundamental Aspect of the Challenge

The fundamental nature of the challenge consists of various confrontation. There are so many situations that are conflicting and intimidating that can cause drawbacks within the lives and minds of people. A considerable portion of this is because of a lack of real teaching, misconceptions, and religious distortions prior to and during the inception of the thought of working in ministry. Intimidations and drawbacks serve to point out shortcomings, disadvantages, problems, downsides, negative aspects, and/or weaknesses.

Many of us experience the intimidation drawback of inadequacy in one form or another. Not one of us is without feelings of inadequacy about or within the self. Biblically speaking, Moses was a splendid example of this. One of the first things that came to his mind was the fact that he would be inadequate for the task of becoming a great deliver because of his drawback, his speech impediment. Many of us feel we have done so poorly in life; perhaps we think we came from the wrong side of the tracks, or maybe we are not educated enough to take on such a tremendous task as ministry work.

However, when we think of the threat we will be to the enemy, we can understand why answering the call would be an issue. We must first understand that recognizing and responding to the call does not come without challenges. None of us enters the ministry unimpeded or untroubled by the enemy, people, and even ourselves.

It is the enemy's goal and or determination to agitate, confuse, and fluster each of us. However, overcoming the challenges as they present themselves will fortify and strengthen us for all that lies ahead. Remember, we are not alone. We are not ill-equipped; "It is for this purpose the Son of God was manifest, that He might destroy the works of the devil" (1 John 3:8).

We are merely the instruments He chose to utilize at this dispensation and time. Now that we have accepted Christ into our lives, we no longer work out of our own abilities and strengths, but it is He who now lives inside and works through us.

We must remember, regardless of our past, what we have or have not done or even our level of education is not a factor when it comes to God's plans and desire for our relationship and purpose in Him. Our thoughts and feelings must reflect:

- If he can use a donkey, surely, He can use me.
- If He can cause rocks rolling downside a mountain to sound like a voice crying out on His behalf, surely, He can utilize me.

- Not of merits of my own, or because of who I am, where I came from, or what I have accomplished, but just because of who He is.
- He is God and God alone.
- He can do anything He desires any way, and anyhow the Lord chooses whenever He chooses.
- Surely, He can utilize my life for His glory.

Because *"we know that all things work together for good to them that love God, to them who are called according to his purpose"* (Romans 8:28, KJV).

Remember, God does not use us as men use one another. Instead, He utilizes that in which He has invested within us. He invested within us special equipping that He, in return, might receive the glory from our lives. The gifts and callings are within us for His purpose, to draw attention to Him, and to gain Him access into our lives and the lives of those we encounter and share Him too.

Making Sure: Our Calling and Election

> Again, Peter states, *"Wherefore the rather, brethren, give the diligence to make your calling and election sure: for if ye do these things, ye shall never fall: For so an entrance shall minister unto you abundantly into the everlasting kingdom of our Lord and Savior Jesus Christ"* (2 Peter 1:10–11 NKJV).

Initially, among the challenges faced is having a relevant understanding of what a calling is. We as believers often find ourselves repeatedly spending much of our time in prayer, fasting, worrying, talking, and searching out various avenues to ensure what our calling or Christian vocation is in life. Because of our constant struggle to identify what our calling is, it is most assuring to know, from the Biblical perspective, a calling is literally a vocation from God.

When we consider acknowledging or recognizing our calling, upon immediately encountering diverse confrontations and challenges, we must realize God is the one who calls and sets apart individuals for ministry work; however, it is required on the part of the individual to ensure his or her own specific calling and election through diligent, careful observation and self-examination.

While at the onset, the various offices may appear to be all "peaches and cream," I assure you that they are not by any stretch of the imagination. Therefore, I encourage everyone endeavoring to venture in these areas to be sure that you are not answering an emotional impulse, an influence passed on to you by someone else, or by the prestige of the office itself. Answering a call from God is not a fly-by-night venture. It is a lifelong endeavor, and those who engage must be committed. Therefore, become fully aware of yourself and your motives before becoming involved in ministry.

In other words, there must be some inner knowledge of who you are. The scripture says, "For many are called, but few are chosen" (Matthew 22:14). There is an adage among some that states, many are:

- Mama called because Johnnie is a good old boy,
- Daddy sent because I paid for his education,
- Then there are those who felt, saw, or heard something, and just got up and went.

Our first scripture admonishes us to "... make your calling and election sure: for if ye do these things, ye shall never fall (2 Peter 1:10). You cannot afford just to go out on another's word. For instance, many may feel an urge to step into a ministerial position because of the prompting of a parent or close friends, which I emphatically do not advise.

However, others such as your spiritual leader(s) or mentor(s) should recognize who you are, especially your pastor(s), who are there to help guide you in this area when and wherever there is a need. It is these individuals who will authorize your position through a license, ordination, appointment, upon entering the ministry. We must always remember that the order of God gives someone else the authority to approve charge in that area.

For those in place to be installed, proclaimed, and consecrated or affirmed upon entrance must also be sanctioned by someone else of equal or higher authority. For instance, bishops are consecrated by a college of bishops. Apostles are affirmed by a conclave of apostles and/

or bishops who function in the office of chief apostles as well. So, even though we as individuals acknowledge our calling into one of the fivefold functioning gifts, someone—our leaders, college, or a conclave—must sanction it.

Often, our gift or calling can be identified through an innate knowing or ability. It is not a fixation or immature obsessing of something you have seen done by others. It is not necessarily something you find yourself struggling with to make fit. It is that which God has gifted us to do or to engage in during our earthly journey. It is that which can be identified by the constant reoccurrence of the same or similar situations, problems, needs, or those things that demand our attention, assistant, or help.

Remember, if you are called out in a ministry, you are being called out for first serving in that ministry. Because you are called does not mean you are fully prepared to leave, go out, and start another ministry on your own. You are subject to those who have the rule over you, those who will authorize you and help and guide you to the place God will utilize you and your gifts most effectively. We are never on our own. Ministry does not work like that. Align with the vision of the house from which you are called and submit to the authority of that house.

Section 6

We Walk By Faith, We Serve By God's Grace

Redeemed by repentance of our sins, we now receive the blessings that God has promised to bestow upon us. We are now the righteousness of God in Christ Jesus our Lord. When we rise in the resurrection, we will receive our reward of righteousness.

Soul winning for Jesus is a delightful part of our duties. As we seek out God's prefect will for our lives, we receive His plan of salvation. While we are sanctifying ourselves from the things of this world, we are saved and are being transformed into saints for God.

Thankfulness to God, who has made our lives possible to live, is a must. He has given us the fruit of temperance and the power to triumph over temptation. He has made it possible to overcome through our testimony. When we are tested and tried, we find His word to be true. He can deliver us through it all. The Lord has given us all that we need to make this journey, and truly we know that if we will taste of Him we will find that He is good (Wooden, 1983).

God Is A God Of Order And Governing Power

Romans 13:1–14

God is the God of order and governing power. This means God alone is our sovereign God. All orders and government come from Him. In other words, we serve a sovereign God, who is our ruler and King. He is the self-directed, self-governing, self-sufficient, Most High, and superior God.

He guides us through and by His providential care and provision. He is the one who alone holds or directs our destiny. He resolves our external circumstances and governs overall outside influences. It is through His divine intervention that our destiny is determined. It is by His directions we live and move and have our very being. It is He by His Son Jesus that makes us the Mantle of Ministry in the five-fold ascension gifts of His calling.

It is He who gives us to understand the significances that we never take credit for God's gifting but to remember that everything that is accomplished is achieved because He utilizes our life to fulfill His purpose and goal. It is by His authorization that Jesus Christ has been invested with all power and authority and that in our putting on the Mantle of Ministry, we are putting on Christ, our hope of glory, God's Son, our sovereign Lord, Savior, and King.

Section 7
WE ARE MOTIVATED TO FOLLOW THROUGH IN GOD'S WORK AND DEEDS!

My encouragement to all is to stay focused and motivated to follow through with God. Your life has meaning and a purpose. Your arrival on planet earth was not in vain. Regardless of all that has occurred previously in your life, you are still important and precious to the Father. It is His will that you become partnered with Him in reaching fallen mankind and helping them to find their way to Him for life eternally. As previously stated,

"**Undefiled** and in union with Christ Jesus, we are bound together by the Holy Ghost and we are in unity with all believers. Virtue flowing in our souls, which was given to us by the power of Christ, has made us victorious in this life.

Wealthy with the riches of the Lord and full of His wisdom, we are witnesses to His wonderful word. Being true worshippers and rendering our all to continue in His will, He has made us worthy of His service through His anointing Spirit, as we wait for that day of His glorious return.

X-rays are the mirrors of our souls. The brightness of Christ is showing through us.

Yearning to follow through in our course, we have yielded completely to God and have taken upon ourselves the yoke of Christ. Zealously we proceed in this current flow of Christianity, in the divine presence of our Supreme Creator" (Wooden, 1983).

More Than Apparel Appeal

Although engaging in ministry has an appealing effect, and while various areas of ministry and leadership positions appear to be glamorous or prestigious from the onset, we should not allow these appeals to become our motivation for becoming a part of the ministry. My advice is, guard your heart with all diligence and avoid getting caught up in the mix.

It is sad to say, many times as outsiders looking in, admiring, and desiring to become what we think we see, we rarely come to know about the internal struggles, ridicules, inner doubts, and bouts with unworthiness that an individual may have endured on his or her way to where he or she appears to be. We, too, often fail to realize that there is a story behind the story. Therefore, it would intrigue us to at least become familiar with the story before leaping head over heels into a situation that may cost us much more than we are willing or able to pay.

This was the situation with Israel choosing a king. The young man Saul was attractive. He looked good, and more than likely, he was a stylish dresser. We as people are often impressed with what we see on the outside and therefore hastily desire to share in the glimmer of the perception we think we see without being fully aware of what it took the individual to get to where he or she is, or even if they thoroughly qualify for being there. However, there is much more to ministry than being attractive and looking good.

Accepting the call to ministry is one of accepting a position of the highest regard. Remember, this is a work of service and of giving glory to God by the good works to which He has called us. Our conduct is not that of self-exhortation, nor is it a position held by overachievers of the more competitive ambitious strivers. Those who have, without a doubt, experienced the call, never take this opportunity for granted.

In fact, we need to know and trust our core values and our place in the Lord. Remembering, displaying Christlikeness, in the way that we conduct ourselves whether privately or publicly, is our goal always. Yes, it is important how we look. Appearance does make a difference. However, what we wear or how attractive we may appear has nothing to do with the power at work from within.

In other words, you can be looking fine and good but not have the power behind your prayers to break the first yoke, or to cast the first demon out of the lives of hurting people. When it comes to the deliverance of a soul, what is inside of you matters the most. It is not how glamorous you look. These things are nice and important in their place but should never become the driving force behind accepting your call to ministry. So, focus on always looking appropriate for the occasion. Remember, you represent others—yourself, family, church, and friends, but most of all, Christ.

Workers Together With Him
Ministers And Conduits Of Grace

2 Corinthians 6: 1–10

Yes, it is more than an apparel appeal. We are workers together with Him Christ, one in the Spirit, and singleness of mind and heart. With that, we must be fully equipped for the assignment ahead.

We are not called to be busybodies, meddling in other people's affairs; we are not gossipers, keeping strife and contention among us, but we hold the words of encouragement, exhortation, enlightenment, and wisdom; we then are the models for others to pattern themselves after.

Yes, we will be misunderstood, at times disliked, ridiculed, and talked about and betrayed by someone we have confided in and trusted. Yes, at times, it will seem hard, and we will become tired of giving our best and keeping to our Biblical instructions and principles, as we do for and share with others while going through our personal trials and affairs in life. Yet, we are not in this alone. After we have stood and withstood, we will know that all things do work together for our good because we love Him and are called according to His purpose.

However, we cannot do any of this in our own strength. We need our Father, the one who has chosen and called us in the inward parts. It is, therefore, extremely necessary to be endowed with His power from on high, which is the Holy Ghost. It is the *Dunamis* power and *Exousia* of that power, which will make the difference in our lives and in the lives of those we encounter.

Our purpose is to serve as ministers and conduits of grace on behalf of God Almighty Himself. Remember, many will look to you and depend on you to be there for them. You must, therefore, "serve wholeheartedly, as if you were serving the Lord, not men" (Eph. 6:7).

The Qualifications Of The Called

The visible representation of the body of Christ in the earth is the body of born-again, baptized believers. Although God is no respecter of persons, (Rom. 2:11, KJV), He does have an order, and he never places anyone in a position without them properly going through the necessary process. The length of time required for going through and qualifying for any call is entirely in the control of God, not man.

The ministry, therefore, is blameless in any way or matter for the mistakes, errors, transgressions, or sins of others. Individuals of the body are accountable and responsible for their own actions and deeds. In fact, in His instructions, we are not to entrust various areas or positions of ministry to a novice, meaning one who has not yet met all the requirements, or is not yet fully prepared for the task.

The Mantle of Ministry or a calling is not manufactured by men but comes from God through the Holy Spirit. Although we can attend classes to understand many of the functions and the operations of ministry, only the Holy Spirit Himself operating through the yielding, willing, obedient believer has the authorization to fulfill God's plans for humankind on the earth. His plans are that we all be edified, built up, and come to our full stature in Him.

Personally, I have not read in any place where God called an individual into ministry without properly preparing them prior to the assignment. From leadership to lay member, we must all prepare before engaging in any area of ministry. Inadequacy is just one of the numerous tactics and maneuvers of the enemy to prevent us from answering or being successful in the call. We should never want to mess up unnecessarily in anything God has entrusted to us. Therefore, it is essential that we become adequately equipped for the task.

Proper preparation, education, and training are designed to intercept the strategies of Satan and to sharpen our awareness of who we are and God's purpose for our lives. Education and training should be a high priority for those who may feel led to enter the ministry. The question is, what does education entail? In simplest of terms, it most definitely includes, but is not limited to:

- A lover of God and His principles
- A student of the Word and of prayer
- An awareness of the times, past, present, and future
- Good standing and relationship with leadership
- A good steward in home affairs, church, and community

An Effective Leader

Crucial Elements of Becoming an Effective Anointed Leader

There are adequate exemplary instances on record for the necessity of preparation for those engaging in ministry, those called to bear the Mantle of Ministry. We take such examples as Moses and Joshua, Elijah and Elisha, Joseph, David, Paul and Jesus, Abigail, Deborah, Huldah and Anna the Prophetess, and many others. Not one of these individuals engaged in the work of the ministry without adequate training or preparation for the office or position of his or her calling. Let us look more closely at the life of some of the above mentioned by way of their tutelage and or the length of their training, such as:

MOSES

I love to reflect on the life, education, strategic training, and experiences of Moses. Moses was born to Hebrew parents during a time when the birth of Hebrew boy babies was being threatened. In the attempt to save his life, Moses's mother, Jochebed, along with the help of his sister, Miriam, devised a well-thought-out plan. They placed the baby in a basket or a little boat and situated him in a vegetated area in the canal of the Nile River, a sacred area where the Pharaoh's daughter usually bathed. Miriam, at a safe distance, kept a watchful eye on the baby to see what the outcome would be.

The Pharaoh's daughter was most likely the sister of Rameses. Seti I was their father and Pharaoh at that time in Egyptian history. Josephus, the renowned Jewish historian, mentions her name as Thermuthis. It has been said that Thermuthis was married but did not or could not have children, and so to come upon Moses, a child owned by no one, was like a precious gift. When the baby was drawn from the river and his clothing was drawn back, he cried. Princess Thermuthis was moved with compassion. She was a woman of influence, position, and power in the empire.

She was the Pharaoh's daughter. Because of her situation of being childless, it was as though a baby had been handed to her, which made her more determined to adopt and raise him. He was now her son and Egyptian royalty.

Although Moses had to endure a forced separation from his family of origin, he was raised by an Egyptian princess in the palace of the Pharaoh. His first form of education was given to him by his birth mother, his nurse, whose identity was most likely not known to the Princess Thermuthis. He learned of the Hebrew religion, faith, and sovereign God and His covenant promise to His people. He was educated in all the history of the then-known world by the most well-versed educators of his time. As a young adult male and son of the Pharaoh, he received military training and other related strategic maneuvers designed for a prince in preparation for leadership positioning.

In other words, for forty years, Moses was educated and went through all the necessary training required for a prince and king of Egypt. After coming to the defense of one of his relatives, and slaying an Egyptian, he became a fugitive in the highlands of Midian. The Midianites were also distant relatives of Moses through Abraham.

It was in Midian that Moses, for the next forty years, learned the how-to of shepherding sheep and the priestly order. Remember, his father-in-law, Jethro, was a Midianite priest and sheepherder. Scripture depicts Moses as being a man well educated, a man of great wisdom in Egyptian affairs; he is known as a mighty or powerful man in words, strategic maneuver, and deeds. He was God's choice to utilize in bringing his people out of bondage and to the Promised Land.

JOSHUA

At some point in time, once Moses returned to Egypt by the divine call of God, he connected with the young man Joshua whom he later mentored. Joshua received his training by Moses for forty years during the wilderness experiences. Joshua received his training, then, anointed, appointed, and assigned, he led the people forward. This marks his calling and positioning in the ministry. He became Moses's successor. The scripture states that after the death of Moses, God spoke to Joshua, saying, "Have not I commanded thee? Be strong and of good courage; be not afraid, neither be thou dismayed: for the LORD, thy God is with thee whithersoever thou goest" (Josh. 1:1–9.

ELISHA

Elisha received his training by Elijah. He did not come into the fruition of his prophetic ministry until twelve years after leaving the field of his father to follow Elijah. He became Elijah's successor. Because of the double anointing upon his life, he was empowered by God to perform double the miracles performed by Elijah during his life, some of which were like those previously performed through his mentor. In other words, He picked right up from where Elijah left off.

JOSEPH

Joseph, the eleventh son of Jacob and the dreamer of dreams, realized the manifestation of his dreams after some thirteen years of betrayal by his brothers. He was hated by his brothers, sold into Egypt, and worked as a hired servant of Potiphar. He was lied about by Potiphar's wife, suffered imprisonment and, finally gained recognition of the Pharaoh to interpret his dream. He became the second greatest man of Egypt, rising to the position of governor.

ABIGAIL

Abigail, a seasoned woman of God (seasoned not meaning old) had applied herself to know and to understand the mind and ways of God. Even King David revered her as a woman of wisdom. After the death of her husband Nabal, she became one of the wives of David and advisor to the King.

JESUS

Jesus Christ, our Lord and Savior, did not exempt Himself from proper training. He first made known His acknowledgment of the call when He was twelve but submitting to the guidance of His parents, He waited for the appointed time, all the while preparing for His earthly ministry. He studied as a rabbi of the Jewish faith, and at the age of thirty, he began his ministry. He further stressed His view of the importance of training by-training His disciples.

The Necessity Of Preparation

People must be prepared or have the necessary instructions before going forth; otherwise, we will make a terrible mess of ourselves. This type of answering to the call is not the bestowing of the Mantle of Ministry and only leads to confusion, misunderstanding, and failure. Those in a leadership position, if not properly prepared, are in a dangerous place that will most likely end in serious misconception with the end resulting in failure.

Sometimes, we receive a sense the call to ministry long before we are ready to walk in it. After the call or acknowledgment of our call, we must then prepare for the calling or assignment, as did those previously mentioned. The protocol or steps of answering the call and entering the ministry consists of, acknowledging the call, and then proving your calling by:

- submitting to leadership,
- applying yourself to study and application in preparation for the call,
- waiting for leadership to position you in your calling or ministry, and most importantly,
- remaining in submission in and in reverence of God.

Therefore, in conclusion of your specific Mantle in Ministry and your embrace of the call, you will proceed in:

1. Knowing Your Mantle of Ministry
2. Areas of Operation in Ministry
3. Positions of Operation within the Church
4. Functioning in Your Position

5. Positions of Operation beyond the Church Walls
6. Knowing Your Best Fit

Entry And Recommended Course Requirements

The following are suggested guidelines to consider for those called to the Mantle of Ministry Embracing the Call and those engaging in various other aspects of ministry.

Let us first address the apostle, the prophet, the evangelist, the pastor, and the teacher. There is a proper protocol for those serving in these offices. First, none of these positions are occupied by a novice. An individual in one of these leadership offices must first know who they are and what they are called to do.

We do not need to add insult to confusion. Have you ever tried taking a rest while someone driving a vehicle is confused about where they are going? The person driving may be a competent driver but is completely lost when it comes to having a sense of direction. Yet, they keep insisting on you resting, and telling you to trust them, saying, I have it. Still every five to ten minutes or so, they are asking you questions about how to get to where they are going. That is an extremely uncomfortable and quite troubling experience. You want your competent driver to be as competent about directions as they are about driving.

That is the same in ministry leadership. People want to feel their leader is competent in who they are and how to get to where they are going. When we look at the Mantle of Leadership, we are looking to people who are competent in their call and clear in how to get us all to the desired destination, which is to our heavenly Father; we are headed home!

The order of entry is based on level of competence. None of the Five-Fold Mantle of Ministry are novices. They each have come through the ranks beginning at the ground floor. Therefore, the apostle is affirmed to apostleship, the prophet is proclaimed to the office of prophet/prophetess, the evangelist is licensed or installed as evangelist, the pastor is installed as pastor, and the teacher is licensed as teacher, and each of these entries should be initiated in a public setting, making an acknowledgment of heaven's call and earth's endorsement.

Then we move to the bishops, overseers, elders, ministers, missionaries, and aspiring missionaries. The bishop is consecrated, the overseer is elevated, the elder is ordained, the minister is licensed, the missionaries are licensed to practice but not permitted to perform weddings and other entitlements of a minister or ordained elder, and the aspiring missionaries are in training.

Also, there are protocol colors and dress codes assigned to each entry level that distinguish one office or position from the other. The general guidelines of Christian liturgical garments and their proper protocol colors for clergy members, are more accurately defined in the diocese you are a part of. It is vitally important to know these protocol vestments and what each item and color represents.

Not to confuse any order of organization previously mentioned in this book, we must respect the fact that not all diocese or organization observe the office of apostles today. Therefore, among the groups that do not, the bishop serves in highest position, except for the Catholic Church, which has its own entirely different set of guidelines and protocols. We will not even attempt to address them here.

Now some may be wondering, how did the position of bishop's override or take the place of highest position in the church versus the apostles? Well that has a history within itself. The position or office of bishop gained prominence when the original apostles and apostolic fathers began to move off the scene. So, with the many struggles within the church and those from without, those in leadership felt a need for individuals who would hold the church to its true teachings, order, and the guidelines that had previously been established.

It was during this period that Irenaeus, who knew Polycarp, who had been a student or prodigy of John, the apostle of Jesus, was made bishop. Under apostolic authority, Irenaeus upheld that after the apostles and apostolic fathers, the bishops offered the safest leadership and accurate clarification of the Word. It is at this period in church history that the bishops began to rise to prominence.

However, as I stated previously, as we read Ephesians 4:11–13, it stands to say, the Mantle of Ministry, embracing the call, still includes the apostle, prophet, evangelist, pastor and teacher, for the edification of the body of Christ. We are still being built up, and we are still being shaped and coming to maturity. All five offices must still be at work, including the apostle because new territories are still be trodden and new works are still being implemented.

All who are answering the Mantle of Ministry by embracing the call, as well as engaging in every phase of effective ministry before receiving a license, ordination, installation, elevation, consecration, proclamation, or affirmation, all must have completed courses in higher education. We must have applied ourselves to the study of God's Word, His principles, ethics, and ways.

There are essential courses that each of us must engage in to perfect ourselves prior to leading others. Our desire should be to always lead others to God, and not be in error, which would lead to failure. The word says, *"Study to shew thyself approved unto God, a workman that needeth not to be ashamed, rightly dividing the word of truth"* (2 Tim. 2:15), KJV).

There is no better way to study and understand the truth than to engage in a full biblical Old and New Testament teaching environment. It is also important that we are aware of current affairs. We cannot get caught up in ancient teachings without understanding how to apply the teachings of the old to the situations of the new. Remember, we are conduits to effect change. The more we study, the more the Father will anoint us to understand and to know his course and His plans. Then He will implement a place and space for you because you applied yourself to know and understand Him.

Now there is no shame to applying yourself to education and the study of God's Word, in a Bible college or institution setting if that institution does not distort the truth of scripture and take away from who God truly is. Courses in Old and New Testament surveys of the Bible, and beyond, Stating Your Identity and Liberty In Christ, How to Understand the Bible, Hermeneutics, The Book of Psalms and how it appeals to all one hundred and twenty or more emotions known to man, and most definitely Public Speaking, as well as in some cases Homiletics.

Take the adventure on the study of the Feast Days of the Bible and how they may still apply today, Ministry Preparation, Church Administration, and so on. Regardless of whatever level we are on, there is always a need for further study for further effective growth. That includes the Five-Fold Mantle of Ministry, embracing the call. For that, we also need:

- ✓ The Attributes and Character of God
- ✓ Homiletics
- ✓ Servant Leadership
- ✓ The Spirit Filled Life
- ✓ Our Foundation of Faith
- ✓ Evangelism
- ✓ Revivalism
- ✓ Church History
- ✓ Spirit Soul and Body
- ✓ Systematic Theology
- ✓ Church and Pulpit and Etiquette
- ✓ Church Protocol
- ✓ Non-Gender Biases neither Male nor Female
- ✓ Communion
- ✓ Funerals
- ✓ Biblical Counseling
- ✓ Angelology
- ✓ Marriage Ceremonies
- ✓ Baptism
- ✓ The Church Structure
- ✓ The Minister's Role in the Church
- ✓ Women in the Bible—Old Testament
- ✓ Women in the Bible—New Testament
- ✓ World Mission
- ✓ Knowing Your Bible (An introduction to the Word of God)
- ✓ World Religion
- ✓ History of Israel
- ✓ Altar Training
- ✓ The Writings of Paul

Entry And Recommended Course Requirements

THERE ARE MANY MORE COURSES TO CONSIDER.

Any of the above areas can be offered through seminars or workshops or through a recommended Bible college, school or ministry or Bible institute as approved by their pastors.

Now in conclusion, we reflect back to the opening scripture and question, *"And I sought for a man among them, that should make up the hedge, and stand in the gap before me for the land, that I should not destroy it: but I found none"* (Ezek. 22:30, KJV).

God is still looking for the ones who will make up the hedge of protection, and the ones who will stand in the gap. He is still looking and calling for the ones who will become the bridge for others to cross from darkness to light. The call is great. Who will answer, and who will properly prepare to be effective in what we are called to do?

www.ingramcontent.com/pod-product-compliance
Ingram Content Group UK Ltd.
Pitfield, Milton Keynes, MK11 3LW, UK
UKHW022222230426
12048UKWH00016BA/1016